United States Army Airborne Patch Guide

ISBN 978-1-884452-23-9 (ebook)
ISBN 978-1-884452-24-6 (POD/SB)

Airborne shoulder sleeve insignia (SSI) are cloth emblems worn on the shoulders of US Army uniforms to identify the primary unit a paratrooper is assigned to. These shoulder sleeve insignia (often abbreviated SSI), are embroidered patches used by Airborne units in the United States Army. Each unit has a unique patch, and the U.S. Army is unique among the U.S. Armed Forces in that all soldiers wear the patch of their assigned unit as part of their military uniforms.

Shoulder sleeve insignia receive their name from the fact that they were most commonly worn on the upper left shoulders of all U.S. Army uniforms, though they can be placed on other locations, notably combat helmets. Shoulder sleeve insignia worn on the upper right shoulders of older Army uniforms denoted wartime service in that unit so it was not to unusual to see a combat veteran of the 82d Airborne Division wearing the patch on both right and left shoulder if serving in the unit later during peacetime.

These "combat patches" are not worn on the new Army Blue Service Uniform. Instead a 2 inch metal replica is worn on the right breast pocket and is officially known as the Combat Service Identification Badge.

Shoulder sleeve insignia generally use intricate designs with bright colors. Because these bright colors and designs stand out when a soldier is in combat, the full color shoulder sleeve insignia is commonly only worn on the dress uniform, when a soldier is not in combat. For combat uniforms, "subdued" versions have been created for wear on the battlefield.

Today unlike previous sew on patches, the Army Combat Unit SSI are Velcro, designed to attach to the Velcro pockets on the shoulder of the uniform, instead of being sewn on. This makes them easier to remove and replace.

Before the new Army Blue service the most common place for the SSI to be worn was on the shoulder of the uniform, however it is also sometimes worn on other places, notably when the soldier's body armor covers the shoulders. SSI are also commonly worn on the shoulder pads of interceptor body armor, which covers the SSI on the uniform. Today, like WW II paratroopers, some soldiers also wear SSI on their Combat Helmets, however this is not standard practice for all units. Some SSI are too large to be worn on the helmets. SSI are also occasionally worn on the backpacks or rucksacks of soldiers, but this is not standard practice and is usually personal preference.

Those soldiers who are combat veterans are authorized permanent wear of the SSI of the unit they fought with on their right shoulder of their ACU. This shoulder sleeve insignia recognizes "former wartime service" and is frequently called a "combat patch".

While this is not a complete display of all airborne patches and their many variations it does cover the majority of US Army airborne units. Please feel free to copy these images for your personal use. The Army does require permission and payment if the images are reproduced for commercial purposes.

Medals of America Press
114 Southchase Blvd
Fountain Inn SC 29644
www.moapress.com

AIRBORNE Armies, Corps and Divisons

 ☐ 1st ALLIED ABN. ARMY

 ☐ 1st ALLIED ABN. ARMY

 ☐ 1st ALLIED ABN. ARMY

 ☐ XVIII ABN CORPS COMBAT ASiGMNT.

 ☐ XVIII ABN CORPS CURRENT ASGN-MT.

 ☐ 8th INFANTRY 1st BRIGADE

 ☐ 8th INFANTRY 1st BRIGADE

 ☐ 9th AIRBORNE *

 ☐ 11th AIRBORNE

 ☐ 11th AIR ASSAULT

 ☐ 13th AIRBORNE

 ☐ 18th AIRBORNE *

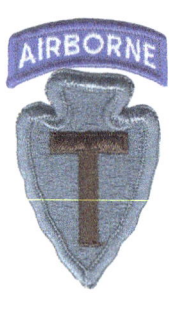 ☐ 71st AIRBORNE BRIGADE

 ☐ 80th AIRBORNE

 ☐ 82nd AIRBORNE

 ☐ 84th AIRBORNE

 ☐ 100th AIRBORNE

 ☐ 101st INFANTRY OLD PATTERN

 ☐ 101st AIRBORNE CURRENT ASSIGNMENT

 ☐ 108th AIRBORNE

AIRBORNE Ground Units and Major Commands

☐ ANTI-AIRCRAFT CMD. - AIRBORNE   ☐ AIRBORNE COMMAND   ☐ U. S. ARMY EUROPE - ABN.   ☐ JOINT READINESS COMMAND   ☐ US ARMY ELEMENT AFRICA COMMAND   ☐ CIVIL AFFAIRS & PSYOPS CMD.

AIRBORNE WW II 'Ghost" Divisons

☐ 6th ABN.   ☐ 9th ABN.   ☐ 18th ABN.   ☐ 21st ABN.   ☐ 135th ABN.

These hollow units were formed on paper in England in 1944. Insignia was designed and worn by individuals in order to convince the Axis spies that there were more troops available for the invasion.

AIRBORNE WW II Army Air Force

☐ AAF - AIRBORNE   ☐ 9th ENGINEER COMMAND (ABN)   ☐ AIRBORNE TROOP CARRIER   ☐ "FLYING BOOT"   ☐ "FLYING FISH"

AIRBORNE Brigades and Combat Teams

☐ 173rd INF. BDE. - ABN.   ☐ 187th R.C.T. 1st DESIGN   ☐ 187th R.C.T. 2nd DESIGN   ☐ 508th R.C.T.

AIRBORNE UNITS

- ☐ PARATROOPS
- ☐ PATHFINDER
- ☐ AIRBORNE INSTRUCTOR
- ☐ RIGGER
- ☐ GLIDERTROOPS

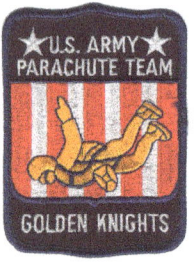    

- ☐ GOLDEN KNIGHTS
- ☐ GOLDEN KNIGHTS
- ☐ GOLDEN KNIGHTS
- ☐ AIRBORNE CMD. - RED TAB
- ☐ ABN. PSYOPS

- ☐ ABN. BOARD H.A.L.O.
- ☐ ABN. SCHOOL SICILY
- ☐ M.A.A.G. AIRBORNE
- ☐ ABN. AERIAL SUPPLY
- ☐ ABN. AERIAL SUPPLY

- ☐ TAB - AIRBORNE
- ☐ TAB - AIRBORNE
- ☐ TAB - AIRBORNE
- ☐ TAB - AIRBORNE
- ☐ TAB - AIRBORNE

- ☐ TAB - AIRBORNE
- ☐ TAB - AIRBORNE
- ☐ TAB - AIRBORNE
- ☐ TAB - AIRBORNE
- ☐ TAB - AIRBORNE

AIRBORNE UNITS

☐ CAP GLIDER - OFF..

☐ CAP GLIDER - E.M.

☐ CAP GLIDER - E.M.

☐ CAP GLIDER - E.M.

☐ CAP GLIDER - E.M.

☐ CAP GLIDER - E.M.

☐ CAP ABN. - E.M.

☐ CAP ABN. - E.M.

☐ CAP ABN. - OFF.

☐ CAP ABN. - E.M.

☐ CAP ABN. - OFF.

☐ CAP ABN. - E.M.

☐ PARATROOPS

☐ GLIDERTROOPS

☐ 3rd ABN PSY-OPS BN.

☐ 3rd AVN BN .- ABN PATHFINDER

☐ 11th ABN DIV. M. P. CO.

☐ 11th ABN DIV.

☐ 11th ABN DIV LRRP BN.

☐ 11th AVN GRP. - ABN PATHFINDER

☐ 17th ABN A.C.R.

☐ XVIII ABN CORPS

AIRBORNE UNITS

- ☐ 24th I.D. - 2nd ABN BDE.
- ☐ 25th MEDICAL DETACH
- ☐ 50th ABN SIGNAL BN.
- ☐ 65th R.C.T. - A CO.
- ☐ 71st ABN BDE.

- ☐ 81st ABN FLD. ARTY. BN.
- ☐ 82nd ABN DIV. 1st BRIGADE
- ☐ 82nd ABN DIV. CMD & CONTROL
- ☐ 82nd ABN DIV. HEADQUARTERS
- ☐ 82nd ABN DIV. SUPPORT

- ☐ 82nd ABN DIV. DIVARTY
- ☐ 82nd ABN DIV. BAND
- ☐ 82nd ABN DIV. SIGNAL BN.
- ☐ 82nd ABN M. I. DET.
- ☐ 82nd ABN F. A. BN.

- ☐ 89th ABN F. A. BATTALION
- ☐ 98th ABN F. A. BATTALION
- ☐ 101st ABN DIV. DIVARTY
- ☐ 101st ABN DIV. SUPPORT UNIT
- ☐ 88th GLIDER INFANTRY REGT.

AIRBORNE UNITS

☐ 101st ABN DIV. A SHAU VALLEY ☐ 101st ABN DIV. AFGHANISTAN ☐ 101st ABN DIV. BASTOGNE ☐ 101st ABN DIV. NORMANDY ☐ 101st ABN DIV. VIETNAM

☐ 101st ABN DIV. 570th POSTAL UNIT ☐ 106th INF. REGT. ☐ 112th ABN SIGNAL BN. ☐ 127th ABN ENGR. BN. ☐ 127th ABN ENGR. BN.

☐ 152nd ABN F. A. BN. ☐ 153rd ABN F. A. BN. ☐ 155th ABN F. A. BN. ☐ 161st ABN ENGR. BN. ☐ 187th ABN INF. REGT.

☐ 187th ABN INF. REGT. ☐ 187th ABN INF. REGT. ☐ 187th ABN INF. MORTAR BN. ☐ 187th ABN INF. MORTAR BN. ☐ 187th ABN INF. REGIMENT

AIRBORNE UNITS

- ☐ 187th ABN INF. L.R.R.P.
- ☐ 187th PARA. GLIDER REGT.
- ☐ 188th ABN INF. REGIMENT
- ☐ 188th ABN INF. REGIMENT
- ☐ 188th ABN INF. REGIMENT

- ☐ 188th ABN INF. REGIMENT
- ☐ 188th ABN INF. REGIMENT
- ☐ 188th ABN INF. REGIMENT
- ☐ 190th GLIDER INF. REGT.
- ☐ 193rd GLIDER INF. REGT.

- ☐ 207th ARCTIC RECON.
- ☐ 221st ABN MEDICAL BN.
- ☐ 265th ABN RADIO RELAY
- ☐ 307th ABN ENGR. BN.
- ☐ 307th ABN ENGR. BN.

- ☐ 313th ABN F. A. BN.
- ☐ 313th M. I. BN.
- ☐ 315th ABN F. A. BN.
- ☐ 319th ABN F. A. BN.
- ☐ 320th ABN F. A. BN.

AIRBORNE UNITS

☐ 321st ABN F. A. BN.   ☐ 325th ABN INF. 2nd BN RECON   ☐ 325th ABN F. A. BN.   ☐ 325th ABN INF. REGIMENT   ☐ 325th ABN INF. REGT.

☐ 325th ABN INF. REGT.   ☐ 326th ABN ENGR. BN.   ☐ 326th ABN F. A. BN.   ☐ 326th ABN MEDICAL CO.   ☐ 326th GLIDER INF. REGT.

☐ 327th ABN F. A. BN.   ☐ 327th ABN INF. REGT.   ☐ 327th PARA INF. - RECON   ☐ 373rd ABN F. A. BN.   ☐ 374th ABN F. A. BN.

☐ 375th ABN F. A. BN.   ☐ 376th ABN F. A. BN.   ☐ 376th ABN F. A. BN.   ☐ 377th ABN F. A. BN.   ☐ 377th ABN F. A. BN.

AIRBORNE UNITS

 ☐ 377th ABN F. A. BN.
 ☐ 401st GLIDER INF. REGT.
 ☐ 426th ABN Q. M. CO.
 ☐ 456th ABN F. A. BN.
 ☐ 457th ABN F. A. BN.

 ☐ 457th ABN F. A. BN.
 ☐ 457th ABN F. A. BN.
 ☐ 457th ABN F. A. BN.
 ☐ 458th ABN F. A. BN.
 ☐ 460th ABN F. A. BN.

 ☐ 460th ABN F. A. BN.
 ☐ 462nd ABN F. A. BN.
 ☐ 462nd ABN F. A. BN.
 ☐ 463rd ABN F. A. BN.
 ☐ 463rd PARA. F. A. BN.

 ☐ 464th ABN F. A. BN.
 ☐ 464th ABN F. A. BN.
 ☐ 465th GLIDER F. A. BN.
 ☐ 472nd ABN F. A. BN.
 ☐ 476th ABN F. A. BN.

AIRBORNE UNITS

☐ 485th GLIDER INF. REGT. ☐ 485th GLIDER INF. REGT. ☐ 501st ABN. INF. REGT. ☐ 501st ABN. INF. REGT. ☐ 501st ABN. INF. REGT.

☐ 501st ABN. INF. REGT. ☐ 501st ABN. INF. REGT. ☐ 501st ABN. SIGNAL BN. ☐ 502nd ABN. INF. REGT. ☐ 502nd ABN. INF. REGT.

☐ 502nd ABN. INF. REGT. ☐ 502nd ABN. INF. REGT. ☐ 502nd ABN. INF. REGT. ☐ 502nd ABN. INF. REGT. ☐ 503rd ABN. INF. REGT.

☐ 503rd ABN. INF. REGT. ☐ 503rd ABN. INF. REGT. ☐ 503rd ABN. INF. REGT. ☐ 503rd ABN. INF. REGT. ☐ 503rd ABN. INF. REGT.

AIRBORNE UNITS

 ☐ 503rd ABN. INF. REGT.
 ☐ 504th ABN. INF. REGT.
 ☐ 504th ABN. INF. REGT.
 ☐ 504th ABN. INF. REGT.
 ☐ 504th ABN. INF. REGT.

 ☐ 504th ABN. INF. REGT.
 ☐ 504th ABN. INF. REGT.
 ☐ 504th ABN. INF. REGT.
 ☐ 504th ABN. INF. REGT.
 ☐ 505th ABN. INF. REGT.

 ☐ 505th ABN. INF. REGT.
 ☐ 505th ABN. INF. REGT.
 ☐ 505th ABN. INF. REGT.
 ☐ 505th ABN. INF. REGT.
 ☐ 505th ABN. INF. REGT.

 ☐ 505th ABN. INF. REGT.
 ☐ 506th ABN. INF. REGT.
 ☐ 506th ABN. INF. REGT.
 ☐ 507th PARA. INF. REGT.
 ☐ 507th PARA. INF. REGT.

AIRBORNE UNITS

 ☐ 507th PARA. INF. REGT.
 ☐ 507th PARA. INF. REGT.
 ☐ 508th ABN. INF. REGT.
 ☐ 508th REGT. COMBAT TEAM
 ☐ 508th ABN. INF. REGT.

 ☐ 508th ABN. INF. REGT.
 ☐ 508th ABN. INF. REGT.
 ☐ 508th ABN. INF. REGT.
 ☐ 508th ABN. INF. REGT.
 ☐ 509th ABN. INF. REGT.

 ☐ 509th ABN. INF. REGT.
 ☐ 509th ABN. INF. REGT.
 ☐ 509th ABN. INF. REGT.
 ☐ 509th ABN. INF. REGT.
 ☐ 509th ABN. INF. REGT.

 ☐ 511th ABN. INF. REGT.
 ☐ 511th ABN. INF. REGT.
 ☐ 511th ABN. INF. REGT.
 ☐ 511th ABN. INF. REGT.
 ☐ 511th ABN. INF. REGT.

AIRBORNE UNITS

 ☐ 512th ABN. INF. REGT.
 ☐ 513th ABN. INF. REGT.
 ☐ 513th ABN. INF. REGT.
 ☐ 513th ABN. INF. REGT.
 ☐ 515th ABN. INF. REGT.

 ☐ 515th ABN. INF. REGT.
 ☐ 516th ABN. INF. REGT.
 ☐ 517th ABN. INF. REGT.
 ☐ 517th ABN. INF. REGT.
 ☐ 517th ABN. INF. REGT.

 ☐ 517th ABN. INF. REGT.
 ☐ 517th ABN. INF. REGT.
 ☐ 518th ABN. INF. REGT.
 ☐ 518th PARA. INF. REGT
 ☐ 519th PARA. INF. REGT.

 ☐ 526th ABN. SUPRT. BN.
 ☐ 541st PARA. INF. BN.
 ☐ 542nd PARA. INF. BN.
 ☐ 542nd PARA. INF. BN.
 ☐ 544th ABN. FLD. ARTY. BN.

AIRBORNE UNITS

 ☐ 549th ABN. FLD. ARTY. BN.
 ☐ 550th ABN. INF. BN.
 ☐ 550th ABN. INF. BN.
 ☐ 550th ABN. INF. BN.
 ☐ 551st PARA. INF. BN.

 ☐ 551st PARA. INF. BN.
 ☐ 551st PARA. INF. BN.
 ☐ 555th PARA. INF. REGT.
 ☐ 555th PARA. INF. REGT.
 ☐ 567th ABN. TRANS. CO.

 ☐ 576th ABN. DEMO. DET.
 ☐ 581st ABN. FLD. ARTY. BN.
 ☐ 596th ABN. ENGR. BN.
 ☐ 596th ABN. ENGR. BN.
 ☐ 674th ABN. FLD. ARTY. BN.

 ☐ 674th ABN. FLD. ARTY. BN.
 ☐ 674th ABN. FLD. ARTY. BN.
 ☐ 674th GLIDER FLD. ARTY. BN.
 ☐ 675th ABN. FLD. ARTY. BN.
 ☐ 680th GLIDER FLD. ARTY. BN.

AIRBORNE UNITS

 ☐ 782nd ABN. MAINT. BN.

 ☐ 801st ABN. ORD. BN.

 ☐ 681st GLIDER FLD. ARTY. BN.

 ☐ 711th ABN. ORD. BN.

 ☐ 877th ABN. ENGR. BN.

 ☐ 905th ABN. FLD. ARTY. BN.

 ☐ 907th ABN. FLD. ARTY. BN.

 ☐ 909th ABN. FLD. ARTY. BN.

US Army Current Active Duty AIRBORNE UNITS

United States Army
United States Army Special Forces
1st Special Forces Group (United States)
3rd Special Forces Group (United States)
5th Special Forces Group (United States)
7th Special Forces Group (United States)
10th Special Forces Group (United States)
19th Special Forces Group (United States)
20th Special Forces Group (United States)
Special Operations Team-Alpha (SOT-A)
Military Information Support Command
4th Psychological Operations Group (United States)
6th Psychological Operations Battalion (USEUCOM)
7th Psychological Operations Battalion (USAFRICOM)
8th Psychological Operations Battalion (USCENTCOM)
8th Psychological Operations Group (United States)
1st Psychological Operations Battalion (USSOUTHCOM)
5th Psychological Operations Battalion (USPACOM)
9th Psychological Operations Battalion (Tactical)
75th Ranger Regiment

XVIII Airborne Corps
82nd Airborne Division
101st Airborne Division
20th Engineer Brigade
4th Brigade Combat Team (Airborne), 25th Infantry Division
173rd Airborne Brigade Combat Team
US Army Long Range Surveillance Companies
US Army Pathfinders Companies
28th Ordnance Company (EOD)(Airborne)

ISBN 978-1-884452-23-9 (ebook)

ISBN 978-1-884452-24-6 (POD/SB)

2016.10.29

www.ingramcontent.com/pod-product-compliance
Lightning Source LLC
Chambersburg PA
CBHW042033100526
44587CB00029B/4406